W9-BRM-427

DEMCO

# GEORGE LUCAS

# GEORGE LUCAS

## Creator of *Star Wars*
by Dana Meachen Rau
and Christopher Rau

A Book Report Biography
FRANKLIN WATTS
A Division of Grolier Publishing
New York / London / Hong Kong / Sydney
Danbury, Connecticut

Cover illustration by Dave Klaboe.
Cover photo by the Gamma Liaison Network © James D. Wilson

Photographs ©: AP/Wide World Photos: 41 (Roger J. Wyan), 27, 77; Archive
Photos: 13 (Michael Barson Collection), 44 (Sam Falk), 89, 96 (Jim Wilson);
Baird Stock Photo: 11, 16; Gamma-Liaison: 49, 62 (Abolafia), 99 (Greg Gor-
man), 100 (Julian Parker), cover (James D. Wilson); Globe Photos: 30 (Ralf
Konow); Kobal Collection: 34, 39, 54, 60, 70, 91; Photofest: 46 (Ralph
McQuarrie Art), 37, 51, 59, 64, 72, 74; Seth Poppel Yearbook Archives: 17;
Sygma: 66 (Tony Korody), 81, (E. Richard), 21 (Ted Soqui), 84 (F. Trapper);
UPI/Corbis-Bettmann: 2, 9; Woodfin Camp & Associates: 23 (Sepp Seitz).

Visit Franklin Watts on the Internet at:
http://publishing.grolier.com

Library of Congress Cataloging-in-Publication Data
    Rau, Dana Meachen, 1971–
    George Lucas : creator of Star Wars / by Dana Meachen Rau and
    Christopher Rau.
        p. cm.—(A book report biography)
    Includes bibliographical references and index.
    ISBN 0-531-11457-0 (lib. bdg.)        0-531-15951-5 (pbk.)
        1. Lucas, George—Juvenile literature. 2. Motion picture producers
and directors—United States—Biography—Juvenile literature. I. Rau,
Christopher. II. Title. III. Series.
    PN1998.3.L835R38      1999
    791.43'0233'092
    [B]—DC21                                                        98-17938
                                                                          CIP
                                                                           AC

© 1999 by Franklin Watts
All rights reserved. Published simultaneously in Canada
GROLIER    Printed in the United States of America
PUBLISHING  1 2 3 4 5 6 7 8 9 10 R 08 07 06 05 04 03 02 01 00 99

# CONTENTS

# CHAPTER ONE

# "WHAT'S GOING ON HERE?"

On May 25, 1977, George Lucas and his wife, Marcia, were on their way to dinner at the Hamburger Hamlet in Hollywood. Lucas was exhausted; he had spent the last two weeks in a dark studio mixing foreign-language versions of *Star Wars.* The next day, he would be on his way to a long-awaited vacation in Hawaii. The lengthy process of creating his space drama was almost over.

Since George was a kid, reading comic books and watching adventure **serials** on television, he had wanted to create a fairy tale in space. After the success of his movie *American Graffiti,* he finally had enough time and money. But it was not easy convincing movie studios that *Star Wars* would be a hit. **Science-fiction** films didn't always do well in theaters, and *Star Wars* was only going to open on thirty-five screens around the United States. But Lucas felt he was creating something that kids, and adults, needed—a modern fairy tale. "There's a whole generation growing up without any kind of fairy tales," Lucas had said. "And kids need fairy tales—it's an important thing for society to have for kids." With *Star Wars*, Lucas had done it. He had created Luke Skywalker—a hero led by an unknown force who battles the dark side and wins.

> **"And kids need fairy tales—it's an important thing for society to have for kids."**

Lucas was so tired from the years of hard work that he had forgotten what day it was—May 25, 1977, the day *Star Wars* was being released. On the way to Hamburger Hamlet, George and Marcia found themselves in a traffic jam. The sidewalks were crowded, too.

"What's going on here?" Lucas asked.

When Lucas turned the corner, he saw where all the people were headed—the Chinese Theater, where the words "Star Wars" were shining in bright lights above the doorway.

The restaurant was right across the street, so George and Marcia pulled in and had dinner. Through the window, George watched fans pour into the theater. He was amazed. Inside, moviegoers were about to visit the new world he had created "a long time ago in a galaxy far, far away."

*Eager crowds line up to see* Star Wars *when it was first released in 1977.*

# CHAPTER TWO

# COMIC BOOKS, TELEVISION, AND RACE CARS

Even multimillionaires and creative geniuses have to start somewhere, and for George Lucas, the starting place was Modesto, California. George's parents, George Walton Lucas, Sr., and Dorothy Bomberger, met in high school in Modesto when they were sixteen years old. They were married less than four years later in 1933.

During the 1930s, America was in the middle of the Great Depression—a time when jobs were hard to find and millions of people were unemployed. Dorothy offered to work, but George Sr. was traditional and wanted to be the sole provider for his family. They settled in Modesto, and George Sr. started working at L. M. Morris, Stationers. Even in that difficult period, he became a successful businessman. Soon the owner sold him half of the business, and eventually George Sr. took over the entire company.

*Lucas grew up in Modesto, California, a town he affectionately remembered later in his films.*

After the birth of two daughters, Katherine and Ann, Dorothy gave birth to George Walton Lucas, Jr. (sometimes called "Georgie"), on May 14, 1944. George's mother was very sick and was frequently hospitalized during his whole childhood. Till, the housekeeper, ran the house and took care of George and his sisters. George and his third sister, Wendy, were inseparable as children.

George's parents were often strict, but Lucas remembers his childhood fondly. George loved their visits to Disneyland. He went camping with the Cub Scouts, swung the bat in Little League, and enjoyed dancing lessons after school.

## ALWAYS LOOKING FOR ADVENTURE

From the time George was little, he always loved to create his own world, like he later would for *Star Wars*. His neighborhood friends, John Plummer and George Frankenstein, helped him set up backyard carnivals, complete with a zoo of pets. George would also surround his train set with elaborate scenes—sometimes whole miniature cities that he built himself.

George loved comic books, which he and Wendy would buy with their allowances. "We had so many that eventually my dad built a big shed in the back, and there was one room strictly devoted to comics, floor to ceiling," George says. His favorite was *Scrooge McDuck*, and he also read *Batman and Robin, Superman, Amazing Stories*, and many

**"There was one room strictly devoted to comics, floor to ceiling."**

others. Luckily for George, John Plummer's father knew the man who owned a local newsstand. So George hoarded the newsman's unsold comics.

After World War II (1939–45), the American economy improved, and the country grew excited

*George spent hours reading comic book stories of his favorite super heroes.*

about a new invention—television. George's father refused to buy a set right away, but John Plummer's father came through for George again. In 1949, Mr. Plummer bought the first television set in Modesto, and George was one of its most faithful watchers. Mr. Plummer even built bleachers in his garage for all of the neighborhood fans. George Sr. finally agreed to buy the family a set of their own. George watched it so much that they put it on a revolving stand so he could watch it from either the kitchen or the living room.

George's favorite show was *Adventure Theater*, with its cliff-hanging endings and nonstop action. He was enthralled by comic book heroes now on television, such as Flash Gordon, who conquered the universe before his very eyes. Television was a major influence on how George would make movies in the future.

## A TEEN OBSESSION

While George was fascinated by his comics and television at home, he was not so thrilled with school. At Roosevelt Junior High School, George remembers, "One of the big problems I had ... was that I always wanted to learn something other than what I was being taught." In class at Thomas Downey High School, he often daydreamed and would only be interested when the teacher showed a film or an educational **documentary**. He did well in art and music, but most of his grades rarely rose above C.

After school, George often went straight to his room to listen to Elvis records, read comic books, eat Hershey bars, and drink Coca-Cola. George was short, skinny, and quiet. He didn't stand out in his classes. His family moved to another house in Modesto when he turned fifteen, and his friends were too far away for just a bike ride.

But George soon became obsessed with a hobby that made him feel powerful and important—where he could shine. He let his hair grow and slicked it back with Vaseline. He wore jeans all the time. He looked tough and he hung out with tough guys. George's father wasn't at all happy with his son. But there was no stopping George. He became obsessed with race cars.

Even before George got his driver's license, he was driving his first car—a Fiat. Soon after he got it, he was speeding so fast that he skidded and flipped the car over. But this gave George the chance to make his Fiat look even more like a sports car. He replaced the bashed-in roof with a roll bar.

George loved racing the broad, flat roads of Modesto. He didn't need to be tall or strong to prove to others and himself that he was good at something. To compete in races, drivers had to be

*George became obsessed with cars. He often cruised to drive-ins to meet friends.*

twenty-one, so George raced and won trophies at smaller autocrosses—contests held in parking lots and fairgrounds—instead. George met and idolized Alan Grant, a champion driver from California, who won every race he entered. George joined racing clubs and became the editor of a club's newsletter. Racing was his life.

In the early 1960s, teenagers with cars didn't just race. They also went cruising. All week, from after school till after midnight, George cruised the streets of Modesto with his friends, looking for girls and blasting rock and roll on their radios. On

*George's high school yearbook photo*

weekends, they cruised all day long. George's experiences provided him with the story and characters for the movie *American Graffiti*, which he would later write and direct.

## GEORGE'S TURNING POINT

George's dream of becoming a race-car driver came to an abrupt end a few days before graduation. On June 12, 1962, George was driving home from the library. He had some term papers to finish, and because of his D average, he wondered if he would even graduate. When he took the left turn that led to his house, a Chevy came out of nowhere and slammed into George's Fiat on the driver's side.

The car flipped four or five times, throwing George through the open roof. George was unconscious as he was rushed to Modesto City Hospital, and his family feared for his life.

Luckily, George pulled through. Looking back, he notes that if his seat belt hadn't released (which it was not supposed to do), he would have certainly been killed. The accident was a turning point in his life. "The fact that I was still alive was a miracle," he

**"The fact that I was still alive was a miracle."**

said. "I realized that I'd been living my life so close to the edge for so long. That's when I decided to go straight, to be a better student, to try to do something with myself."

Instead of pursuing a career with cars, George decided to go to college. His high school diploma was delivered to his hospital room three days after the accident, but his grades weren't good enough to gain entrance to a four-year school. So his next step was Modesto Junior College.

# CHAPTER THREE

# A LEGEND AND STAR IS BORN

Modesto Junior College couldn't begin to match the excitement of racing and cars, and at first Lucas fell asleep over his books. But as he started learning things that interested him, such as sociology, anthropology, literature, and creative writing, his grades began to improve. He still devoted his spare time to cars, but he also began experimenting with a friend's 8-mm movie camera.

On June 9, 1964, Lucas graduated from Modesto Junior College with an associate in arts degree. While Lucas decided what to do next, his childhood friend, John Plummer, suggested that Lucas apply to the University of Southern California (USC) in Los Angeles. While helping build a race car, George got to know its owner, Haskell Wexler, an important Hollywood **cinematographer**. Wexler liked Lucas right away, and he may have helped Lucas get accepted to USC's film school.

*Cinematographer Haskell Wexler (shown here in 1996) took an interest in Lucas.*

## LAUNCHING A CAREER

George Lucas, Sr., was not happy with George's choice to pursue a career in the movie industry. He wanted George to take over the family business at L. M. Morris. They often argued, and during one of their quarrels, George vowed to his father that he would be a millionaire before he turned thirty.

Even though George frequently disagreed with his father, George Sr. taught him important character traits that helped him for his entire life—strong morals and principles, honesty, and the value of hard work. Still, George Sr. was not comfortable paying George's way through college. Instead, they agreed that George Sr. would pay him a salary to be used as tuition. He wanted his son to think of college as a job, and if he didn't work hard at it and do well, he could come home and work for L. M. Morris.

From the day Lucas entered USC as a junior, teachers described him as a determined and promising student. While other students were dismayed at the obstacles USC put in their way, George was up for every challenge. "When I got to film school, the other students said, 'You really can't make movies here. They don't give you enough film, they don't let you keep the camera for very long.'" George said. "Well, I made eight films at USC. . . . It was difficult, and there were lots of barriers, but it wasn't impossible."

Because Lucas had to catch up to other students who had already taken film classes in their freshman and sophomore years, he worked nonstop. Plummer remembers how hard his friend worked: "This was a guy who never had any direction before, and now suddenly he had asserted himself and became totally devoted to one thing, film." Lucas, too, remembers that in college, "my whole life was film—

**"My whole life was film—every waking hour. It was all new, neat, and exciting."**

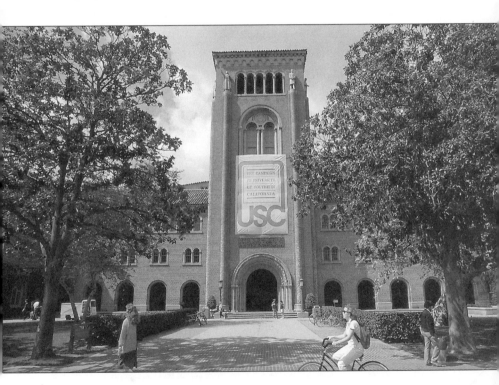

*At USC, Lucas threw himself into studying and creating films.*

every waking hour. It was all new, neat, and exciting." He and his friends went to the movies all the time, sometimes seeing as many as five films in a weekend.

## BREAKING THE RULES

Students at USC had to complete two assignments—a black-and-white project that had to be filmed within five weeks, and a longer, ten-week project. Very few students completed the five-week project, and even fewer finished the ten-week film. But Lucas never had that problem. He not only finished the five-week project, he tacked on a trailer of coming attractions for his longer movie. Lucas said that "the department never taught us much, other than the basics. They opened the door, but we had to go inside and find out for ourselves. . . . Whenever I broke the rules, I made a good film, so there wasn't much the faculty could do about it."

**"Whenever I broke the rules, I made a good film, so there wasn't much the faculty could do about it."**

In making his student movies, he developed a style that would stick with him throughout his career. His movies had lots of action, good sound, short dialogue, and a fast pace, much like the comic books he loved as a boy. He liked to control all aspects of his movies, but one of his favorite roles was as the **editor**. He believed that the shooting of the film didn't control how it would come out, but the way it was edited and rearranged made the movie come together. Some of Lucas's student films include *Look at Life, Herbie, Freiheit, The Emperor*, and *1:42:08* (about auto racing).

Lucas was becoming the envy of other young filmmakers. Steven Spielberg remembers, "George Lucas was always the star of the student film festivals then." But Lucas was not the only "legend" being born in film schools in the mid-1960s. A whole group of young filmmakers was emerging from film schools all over the United States—Steven Spielberg from Long Beach State, Francis Ford Coppola from UCLA, Brian De Palma from Columbia University, and Martin Scorsese from New York University.

## FINDING A WAY INTO HOLLYWOOD

Lucas graduated from USC on August 6, 1966, with a bachelor of arts degree in cinema. The United States was involved in the Vietnam War at the time. Lucas was against the war, but he was drafted. When he went for his physical, however, the doctors discovered that he had **diabetes**.

While the disease would trouble him throughout his life, the rejection from the armed services gave Lucas the freedom to pursue his career at the age of twenty-two.

Lucas started looking for a job in the movies. Verna Fields, a film editor, hired him to work for the United States Information Agency (USIA) on educational and propaganda films as an assistant **grip**. Fields also hired Marcia Griffin to work as an assistant editor. Lucas and Griffin became friends, even though they were very different. Lucas was still a shy, awkward student, and Griffin was a career-minded woman who already knew a lot about the industry. But they were both born in Modesto, and they both loved film. They often went on dates to the movies, and on February 22, 1969, they were married.

Lucas returned to USC as a graduate student for one semester in 1968. He worked all week for USIA, and spent his nights and weekends directing another 15-minute student film, *THX 1138:4EB* about a man trying to escape from a futuristic society. It had elements never seen in a student film before, such as traveling shots and sophisticated graphics. The people at USC were not the only ones who noticed the value and innovations of the film. So did Hollywood.

Lucas was one of three students awarded a Columbia Pictures scholarship to direct short

*Lucas and his wife, Marcia*
*(at the Academy Awards in 1978)*

films of the making of *McKenna's Gold*, a Western adventure filmed in Arizona. But what launched his career was another scholarship offered by Warner Brothers in 1968. As the winner, Lucas could observe the making of a film for six months.

At the time, the only production shooting on the Warner Brothers lot was a musical called *Finian's Rainbow*, with Francis Ford Coppola as **director**.

Coppola was already a legend in the film-student community. "We started a conversation and a friendship," Coppola says about their meeting on the lot. After the scholarship ended, Lucas had intended to go back to USC to finish his master's degree, and then perhaps move to San Francisco to direct commercials and educational films. But he saw possibilities with Coppola, and when Coppola began to film his next project, *The Rain People*, Lucas joined the **crew**.

# CHAPTER FOUR

# LUCAS VERSUS HOLLYWOOD

From the beginning, Coppola was a major influence on Lucas's career. But Lucas was not content with just observing Coppola. On the set of *The Rain People*, Lucas filmed his own documentary—*Filmmaker*—which focused on Coppola. Coppola was only five years older than Lucas, but he represented what Lucas wanted to achieve. "I was very grateful to have someone of my own generation around to discuss what I was trying to do," Lucas once said.

Coppola was loud, burly, and a risk-taker, while Lucas was quiet and more cautious. Lucas admits that he and Coppola "were like two halves of a whole. I was always putting on the brakes and he was always stepping on the

**"I realized that you can jump off the cliff and survive 99 percent of the time."**

*Francis Ford Coppola gave Lucas*
*valuable support and friendship.*

gas. It was good for me, because it loosened me up and got me to take more chances. I realized that you can jump off the cliff and survive 99 percent of the time."

## AMERICAN ZOETROPE

While Coppola and Lucas were very different in personality, they had a similar vision of how movies should be made. Both of them were disgusted at the way Hollywood worked. They wanted to make movies in an environment where filmmakers were encouraged to take chances that the Hollywood studios would never risk. So they created a company of their own, American Zoetrope, of which Coppola was sole shareholder, and Lucas was vice president. (A zoetrope is a device that projects moving images as its cylinder is spun.) At the company's formation, its announcement read: "The essential objective of the company is to engage in the varied fields of filmmaking, collaborating with the most gifted and youthful talent using the most contemporary techniques and equipment possible."

Lucas and Coppola disagreed on the perfect setting for their company. Coppola wanted a grand studio, and Lucas wanted "a nice little house." However, when they found an available warehouse in downtown San Francisco in 1969, they moved in. American Zoetrope was up and running, and soon it was filled with ultramodern editing equipment and a staff of creative young filmmakers.

To get American Zoetrope off the ground financially, Coppola presented seven movie projects to Warner Brothers. One of these projects was a feature-film version of Lucas's student film *THX 1138:4EB*. Warner Brothers agreed to give American Zoetrope $3.5 million to develop scripts for five of the seven projects, including *THX 1138:4EB*.

As Lucas began working on adapting his student film for the big screen, he found that the script wasn't coming together. Lucas considered leaving it for a while and focusing his attention on *Apocalypse Now*, a project about the Vietnam War he had conceived with John Milius, a friend from college. But Coppola wasn't ready to leave *THX 1138:4EB* behind. He went to Warner Brothers with footage from the first *THX 1138:4EB* and the idea for *Apocalypse Now*, and Warner agreed to take on both projects.

## THE STRANGE WORLD OF *THX 1138*

Lucas's salary for writing and directing the newly named *THX 1138* was only $15,000, but it was a great opportunity to be as creative as he wanted. "I realized that I might never get the chance again to make this totally off-the-wall movie, without any real supervision."

He was given a ten-week shooting schedule—the same time he was given for his student film. *THX 1138* was a "science-fiction documentary" according to Lucas. The setting is in an underground, computerized, drug-controlled society in the twenty-fifth century. Lucas shot the film in the subway tunnels and parking garages of Los Angeles. His cast included Robert Duvall as the lead character.

Lucas had a year to work on the **postproduction**, which he did at American Zoetrope, so he had been involved in all parts of the movie—the writing, the directing, and the editing. He was pleased that he could control his vision of *THX 1138* from start to finish.

But he came up against the cruel realities of Hollywood when he handed the finished film to Warner Brothers. They thought the final film was too strange and ordered Coppola and Lucas to turn the movie over to their in-house editor, who would re-edit the film. Warner Brothers was so upset about *THX 1138* that they actually canceled the entire deal they made with American Zoetrope and refused to consider the other projects. "They told Francis we were going to have to pay back all the money they'd advanced," Lucas says. "It was a dire time." American Zoetrope never recovered from this blow so early in its history.

*This scene from* **THX 1138** *demonstrates
the fantastic world of Lucas's imagination.*

Lucas was especially distraught. Warner Brothers ended up cutting only four minutes from the film, but Lucas had been proud of *THX 1138*, and it had been taken away from him. "The cuts didn't make the movie any better; they had absolutely no effect on the movie at all," he says. "It was a very personal kind of film, and I didn't think they had the right to come in and just arbitrarily chop it up at their own whim."

> **"It was a very personal kind of film, and I didn't think they had the right to come in and just arbitrarily chop it up."**

*THX 1138* came out in 1971 to mixed reviews. Some critics thought it was depressing and even "tedious." But most praised the atmosphere and action and recognized Lucas's creative use of technology. A reviewer for *Newsweek* in 1971 called *THX 1138* "an extremely professional first film." *THX 1138* was Lucas's biggest commercial failure, but he remembers it as one of his favorite films.

After *THX 1138*, Lucas says that he and Coppola "had to go our separate ways." Coppola started his next movie, *The Godfather*. Lucas worked a little more on *Apocalypse Now*, but couldn't find a studio. So he started to develop a screenplay for his second feature film—one that would finally put him on the map.

# CRUISING AGAIN WITH *AMERICAN GRAFFITI*

After *THX 1138*, Lucas feared that he had gained a reputation as "a cold, weird director, a science-fiction sort of guy who carried a calculator. And I'm not like that at all. So, I thought, maybe I'll do something exactly the opposite."

Lucas's idea for *American Graffiti* was the story of one summer night in 1962 as four teenage boys, who have just graduated from high school, cruise through the streets of town, pick up girls, and race cars. It was based on Lucas's own teenage years in Modesto. "It all happened to me, but I sort of glamorized it," Lucas said in a *New York Times* interview. "I went through all that stuff, drove the cars, bought liquor, chased girls. I think a lot of people do, which is the whole idea behind the title—a very American experience."

The major studios rejected the idea, mainly because getting the rights for all the songs Lucas wanted in the film would be too expensive. United Artists showed some interest, and Lucas went straight to the president, David Picker, who offered him $10,000 to develop a script. But the two writers Lucas most wanted to help him write it—Gloria Katz and Willard Huyck—were working on a horror movie. Lucas wrote several drafts himself. United Artists rejected the movie, as did all the other major Hollywood studios.

*Lucas based his characters in* American Graffiti *on American teenagers of the fifties. Ron Howard and Cindy Williams (above) were two of the movie's stars.*

When Lucas was finally able to get Katz and Huyck to join the project as writers, Universal agreed to take the film. But they made certain conditions, because they didn't want it to be a big risk for their studio. They wanted Coppola to produce it because it was rumored that *The Godfather* was going to be a huge hit. (Coppola agreed to work as co-producer with Gary Kurtz, who actually did most of the work on the film.) They also wanted the film to be done cheaply and quickly—they gave Lucas a budget of only $750,000 and a shooting schedule of just twenty-eight days.

Lucas got to work. First he found a stellar cast. Future stars, such as Ron Howard, Richard Dreyfuss, Cindy Williams, Suzanne Somers, and Harrison Ford, made up the group of young characters. But the rest of the film was not that easy. As expected, most of the film's budget had to pay for rights for the soundtrack. Lucas had originally suggested that eighty songs be included. Universal pressured him to use only five. Lucas settled on forty-five. To Lucas, music was vital to the film's story.

Lucas had to shoot *American Graffiti* at night, which caused some problems. Night shooting had not even been technologically possible just a few years earlier, so Lucas's shooting methods had not been greatly tested. Modesto didn't work as a location for shooting, so Lucas chose San Rafael. He paid the town $300 a night to

*Cars were another important part of the*
American Graffiti *story.*

shoot there. Soon after, a local business com-
plained, and they had to move the shooting to
Petaluma. They also needed four hundred cars
popular in the 1950s and 1960s, so the crew paid
car owners $25 a night to bring their automobiles.

When he finished shooting, George wanted
Marcia to edit the film. Universal chose the more

experienced Verna Fields to work with her. It was a challenging job—the stories of four different characters had to be interwoven throughout the film, with music as the framework. Finally, it was ready for a preview.

At this point in his career, Lucas was flat broke. To help with his taxes, he set up a company he called Lucasfilm Ltd. At the preview of *American Graffiti* in January 1973, he looked on with pride as the Lucasfilm Ltd. logo appeared on screen for the first time. He was even more thrilled when the audience loved the movie.

The executives at Universal did not like the film, however, and they wanted to make cuts. In the back of the theater after the preview, Coppola, with his typical passion, shouted at the executives, demanding to buy the film from them to protect its integrity. The film stayed with Universal, and they cut only five minutes from the movie before it was released in August 1973. But Lucas was extremely frustrated. He was experiencing the same problems he had faced with *THX 1138*. "They wanted it shorter . . ." Lucas said, "so they cut five minutes out of it, and I was furious."

> **"They cut five minutes out of it, and I was furious."**

Even with the cuts, *American Graffiti* was a huge hit. It was nominated for five Oscars and

*In 1997, the town of Modesto honored Lucas by
building a statue of a scene from* American Graffiti.

stayed in theaters for two years. It grossed $50 million, and because it had cost the studio only $750,000 to make, it earned one of the biggest profits in history. Reviews hailed *American Graffiti* for "bringing the past alive." The *Los Angeles Times* called it "one of the most important films of the year." Lucas had created a film that depicted an experience common to teenagers across America, not only those in Modesto. Everyone cruised, everyone loved the rock-and-roll songs, and everyone could relate to the movie.

*American Graffiti* gave Lucas a reputation as a first-rate director and also launched his next, and most-unexpected, success. Lucas was ready to start work on a rough idea for a space drama that would grow into *Star Wars*.

# CHAPTER FIVE

# THE FORCE

After *American Graffiti*, Lucas was no longer broke. In fact, he beat his goal of becoming a millionaire by the time he was thirty by two years. His lifestyle didn't really change, but he made one important purchase—a Victorian house in Marin that became the home of Lucasfilm Ltd. The bedrooms were turned into offices for the staff, and Lucas had a separate office where he could work on the script for *Star Wars*.

## WRITING THE CLASSIC TALE

Lucas worked hour after hour, day after day, to create the story that fans have come to know and love. His original draft started off with basic settings, such as a desert, a jungle, and a strange city in the clouds. Lucas spent a lot of his time researching science-fiction and fantasy stories, as

*After the success of* American Graffiti, *Lucas was ready to create a new film about a war among the stars.*

well as myths from all over the world. He even went back to reading comic books. While Lucas pulled ideas from many traditional sources, he made his story into something unique. By 1974, he had completed the first draft of a screenplay.

In a recent interview, Lucas remembers that he thought *Star Wars* might be "too wacky for the general public. I just said, 'Well, I've had my big hit [with *American Graffiti*], and I'm happy. And I'm going to do this crazy thing, and it'll be fun.'" But even though the success of *American Graffiti* had given Lucas the freedom to work on his great fantasy epic, time was not unlimited. After creating a basic script, Lucas searched for a studio to back the project. In spite of its large profits from *American Graffiti*, Universal turned Lucas down. So did United Artists. Twentieth-Century Fox showed some interest, but Lucas couldn't find an enthusiastic response anywhere. He felt that the studio executives didn't understand his vision for the film. Perhaps his previous science-fiction film *THX 1138* had scared some of them off.

By 1975, Lucas had completed the screenplay to the middle portion of a giant space epic. Lucas hired Ralph McQuarrie, a commercial illustrator, to create pictures to bring his vision to life. (McQuarrie was also responsible for design work on some other famous projects, such as *E.T.: The*

*Artist Ralph McQuarrie painted this scene from*
Star Wars *for Lucas to show to movie producers.*

*Extra-Terrestrial* and *Cocoon*.) Lucas and his producer, Gary Kurtz, provided McQuarrie with a
script. But Lucas didn't want just sketches—he
wanted finished paintings. McQuarrie remembers, "He wanted people to look and say, 'Gee, that
looks great, just like something on the screen.'"

Soon, they had five paintings to show the executives what Lucas's strange new world might look like. Twentieth-Century Fox producers liked what they saw and gave Lucas some start-up money to expand the project. After McQuarrie painted even more pictures, the studio bought into the project and decided to support its completion. Lucas's dream of making *Star Wars* a movie was finally coming true.

Lucas soon realized that even this small part of the bigger story he had proposed was much too long for one movie. He divided the *Star Wars* story into three episodes and set the second two aside. The whole story would take several movies.

Lucas wanted to be sure the sequels would have a chance to be made. One of the most important parts of Lucas's negotiations with 20th-Century Fox was his agreement to give up a good portion of his director's fee in exchange for the sequel and merchandising rights from *Star Wars*. In the 1970s, this seemed like a great deal for the studio. Sequels were far off in a distant and very unsure future, and almost no money was ever made from movie merchandise. In the eyes of the studio, Lucas had sacrificed a lot of money. But no matter what occurred with *Star Wars*, Lucas did not want to lose control of his story. When he set the other two parts of the story aside to make *Star Wars*, he said, "I will get back to you. I will see to it that you get made."

Lucas's vision was large from the beginning. *Star Wars* was not just a science-fiction movie. Lucas had no doubt that he was filling a void in Hollywood: "When I created the original *Star Wars*, I was very interested in creating a modern myth to take the place that had been occupied by the Western. . . . Greek mythology, or mythology from any country, often takes place in an unknown area, but one that is believable to the audience. The only area we have now that is like that is outer space. So I decided outer space was a good idea."

> "When I created the original *Star Wars*, I was very interested in creating a modern myth."

## PROBLEMS WITH PRODUCTION

Lucas needed to find a cast. He wanted fresh, unknown actors to star in the movie. After an exhaustive screening for the three leads, he chose Carrie Fisher as Princess Leia, Harrison Ford as Han Solo, and Mark Hamill as Luke Starkiller. (His character's name wasn't changed to Luke Skywalker until the first day of shooting.) Mark Hamill remembers the grueling casting process for his pivotal role, "There were guys literally everywhere, in age from sixteen to thirty-five."

*For* Star Wars, *Lucas cast Mark Hamill as Luke Skywalker (left); Carrie Fisher as Princess Leia (center); and Harrison Ford as Han Solo (right).*

Although Ford had been in *American Graffiti,* he was not yet a star, and Fisher and Hamill had almost no experience in films. The studio was not pleased. Ford recalled that "George wanted and hired strong personalities." Lucas managed to gather the studio's support, however, when he signed the gifted and experienced Alec Guinness to play Obi-Wan Kenobi.

Another problem Lucas faced was trying to create his new world. For the desert scenes, Lucas started to shoot in Tunisia, Africa, in March 1976. The crew was scheduled to spend only eleven days there, and only Hamill and Guinness had made the trip to shoot scenes. It was bitterly cold in the desert, and the strong winds of sandstorms often knocked over the sets. Everyone had to wear goggles to protect their eyes from the sand. R2-D2's electronic controls didn't work, and he kept falling over. And Anthony Daniels, the actor inside C-3PO, had trouble moving around in his suit. Shooting threatened to go many days past schedule, and the budget did not allow for these early setbacks. In a letter to his wife, Lucas expressed his frustration, "I forget how impossible making movies really is. I get so depressed, but I guess I'll get through somehow." In the end, the crew's hard work paid off. With only a few hours of sleep each night, the crew managed to get most of the shots Lucas wanted.

> **"I forget how impossible making movies really is. I get so depressed."**

*Lucas (second from left) and his film crew
struggle to shoot the first scenes of* Star Wars
*in the Tunisian desert.*

Most of the film was made in England at
Elstree Studios outside London. Elstree had many
sound stages, and it was cheaper to make movies
in England than in the United States. Lucas's
style came through during filming. He always

wanted things to be "faster and more intense." But even though shooting in England was easier than shooting in Tunisia, Lucas still had problems. Time limits put immense pressure on Lucas and the crew.

In the meantime, his crew was finding that *Star Wars* was a unique experience. "My first impression was that he [Lucas] was an average sort of guy," says Peter Meyhew, the giant actor inside Chewbacca's furry suit. "He didn't look like the image of a Hollywood director." Harrison Ford especially appreciated George's style, "Very little time was wasted. George didn't have an authoritarian attitude like many directors. . . . He was different. . . . He encouraged our contributions."

> **"He was different. . . . He encouraged our contributions."**
> —Harrison Ford

Lucas had to make many trips from England back to the United States to coordinate the other major part of the movie with a company he had created the year before—Industrial Light and Magic.

## THE NEED FOR SPECIAL EFFECTS

Lucas had to create his own **special effects** studio, because no studio in Hollywood could handle all the effects needed for *Star Wars*. Starting in the 1920s, large movie studios built complete production facilities—including special-effects shops. But in the 1950s, studios became less powerful and there were many more independent filmmakers. No longer were a few studios in control of the entire motion-picture industry. So when it was time to put *Star Wars* together and he needed a special effects studio, Lucas opened Industrial Light and Magic (ILM) in a warehouse in Van Nuys, California.

Lucas hired John Dykstra as the person in charge of special effects, and Dykstra hired the staff for ILM. At that time, very few people had experience working with special effects. So instead of hiring professionals, Dykstra hired young, energetic people who knew a lot about computers and how they could be used for effects. (*Star Wars* was the first feature movie to use a computer to control the special-effects camera.) Dykstra hired technicians to build film equipment, computer geniuses to come up with ways in which computers could control the models, artists to design spacecraft and monsters, and model builders to make everything look real.

ILM was unlike any Hollywood studio. Most of the technicians working there were under thirty years old, and some were even under twenty. It was a casual, relaxed place to work, with no dress

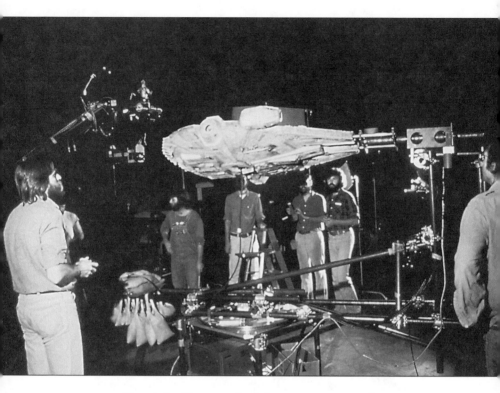

*Special-effects technicians prepare a shot of Han Solo's ship, the* Millenium Falcon.

code or specific working hours. But the people at ILM worked hard and felt that they were part of something very important.

Along with all the special effects, Lucas also needed believable sounds and inspiring music to complete the movie. A whole new department of ILM was created to deal with the many sound effects—from using angry walruses for the sound of Chewbacca's voice to recording hammers hitting antenna wire for the laser blasts. Also, Lucas hired Academy Award-winning John Williams to create a **score** that would fit Lucas's great myth. Lucas wanted a classical sound and Williams suggested, "Why don't you let me write our own classical music?" He created a momentous score, where each character had a theme in the music.

## THE SUCCESS OF *STAR WARS*

Lucas and his entire crew were completely exhausted when *Star Wars* finally opened in 1977. Even now, Lucas says that making *Star Wars* "wasn't very much fun." And when the movie was ready for release, Lucas did not think it would be a huge success. He just hoped it would make back the money the studio had invested. It opened on only thirty-five screens, but before long it was showing all over the country. Many people, in a time before VCRs, went to see the movie more than one hundred times.

*Star Wars* not only made back the money it cost to make the film, it became one of the most successful movies in history. The song "Star Wars: The Cantina Band" was at the top of the pop single charts all summer. Star Wars merchandise could be found everywhere—from lunch boxes to action figures to novels. Lucas created his own division, LucasArts Licensing, to handle the merchandise profits. *Star Wars* was nominated for ten Academy Awards and won five—best art and set direction, best costume design, best original score, best visual effects, and best film editing, which went to Lucas's wife, Marcia. And Lucas shared profits with not only the cast and crew, but with all of his employees—even the housekeeping staff at ILM.

After the unbelievable success of *Star Wars*, Lucas gained a level of control over his movies that very few people in Hollywood enjoy. Lucas never doubted that he would make a sequel. Because *Star Wars* had been so profitable, he was able to negotiate an incredible deal with the studio that let him keep a large percentage of the profits along with merchandising and creative control.

## MORE AMERICAN GRAFFITI

Lucas was ready to dive into working on the *Star Wars* sequel, *The Empire Strikes Back*, but he had to work on another project at the same time. Universal Studios wanted to make a sequel to *American Graffiti*. Lucas didn't wish to write or direct it, but he didn't want to give up control. Universal owned the characters, so Lucas wanted to make sure the sequel was true to the characters he had created.

The story of *More American Graffiti* follows the same characters in the 1960s, including their experiences racing cars and in the Vietnam War. Lucas saw working on the movie as a chance to experiment and try new film techniques. Certain sequences showed Lucas's fine skill at editing. For example, they had filmed only two helicopters landing, but when Lucas was through with the film, there appeared to be a dozen.

Unfortunately, *More American Graffiti* was a commercial failure. The film had not been a continuation of the fun, carefree life of teenagers portrayed in *American Graffiti*. Instead, it dealt with drugs, death, war, and sex, subjects that audiences did not associate with the man who created *Star Wars*.

## STRIKING BACK

When Lucas started work on *The Empire Strikes Back* in 1978, he felt a lot of pressure because his other attempt at a sequel (*More American Graffiti*) had failed. But *Star Wars* fans around the world could hardly wait to find out what happened to their favorite characters.

**"I was very nervous when I started the second film."**

Since the story was the middle story of three, Lucas knew the film was headed for some dark, dramatic moments. "I was very nervous when I started the second film," he admitted. He was concerned the fans might feel let down.

Lucas worked on the screenplay himself, but he knew it needed work. He hired Lawrence Kasdan, who wrote a draft for *The Empire Strikes Back*. (Kasdan also wrote *Raiders of the Lost Ark*.) The story was ready for filming by early 1979.

Lucas had completely exhausted himself making *Star Wars* and decided he could not play every role in the making of *Empire*. "As a director, I wanted to do everything," he said. "It's very hard for me to delegate things to other people. Well, the best way to do that is to take one more step back and be forced to delegate everything. And see if I could stand it." Lucas became executive producer and hired Irwin Kershner to direct the film. It was very difficult for Lucas to give up control. He felt "Chewbacca is still my Wookie and R2-D2 is still my little robot." But it was necessary if he was going to survive the process.

For the most part, the rest of the *Star Wars* team was brought together again for the making of *Empire*. They made the movie in three places— Norway for the scenes on the ice planet of Hoth, Elstree Studios in London, and California at ILM. Lucas spent most of his time in California working on the technical side of the film.

Lucas had very little trouble convincing the original cast to return. Ford and Fisher had

*To create* The Empire Strikes Back, *Lucas (second from right) hired Irvin Kershner to direct (far left); Gary Kurtz as executive producer (second from left); and Lawrence Kasdan to prepare the screenplay (far right).*

become much more famous since the making of *Star Wars*, and both of them, along with the rest of the cast, saw *The Empire Strikes Back* as a chance to return to the roles that made them stars. Lucas also added several new characters—

*Filming a scene of* The Empire Strikes Back

Yoda and the Emperor brought more definition to the mysterious Force that Obi-Wan had introduced in *Star Wars*. Lando Calrissian, an old friend of Han Solo's and the owner of Cloud City, was also introduced.

Like *Star Wars*, many problems arose during filming. Kershner was under constant pressure to speed up and keep costs down. There was also a conflict between the Lucas and Kershner styles. Eventually Lucas was able to step back and let Kershner control the making of the film. But Lucas's constant travel between California and London made the second *Star Wars* as tiring as the first. Throughout the filming, Lucas worked on editing the film to fit his vision.

By the time *The Empire Strikes Back* was completed, Lucas had spent $33 million of his own money. When he saw the finished product, he was not convinced it would match the success of *Star Wars*. But the movie ended up making $365 million worldwide. Lucas got back every cent he had invested along with a huge profit.

## THE LEGEND RETURNS

On May 25, 1983, six years to the day after the release of *Star Wars*, *Return of the Jedi* appeared on the big screen. With this second sequel, Lucas completed the middle **trilogy** of his grand nine-

*Darth Vader is one of the most recognizable villains in movie history.*

picture epic. He also gave his fans a brighter conclusion than they had with *The Empire Strikes Back*. In *Return of the Jedi*, the powers of good finally achieved a solid victory in their war against the evil Empire.

With *Return of the Jedi*, Lucas used the formula that had been so successful in the first two movies. He blended an amazing story with interesting characters and special effects that had never been attempted before. In *Jedi*, Lucas added the Ewoks, a small, teddy-bear-like tribe of natives who lived in wooden huts in the middle of a forest. (Lucas had originally intended this group of creatures in *Jedi* to be Wookies, but he liked them so much that he created the Wookie character of Chewbacca for *Star Wars*.) These small, almost childlike Ewok creatures were caught in the middle of a battle with the all-powerful Empire.

In some ways, *Return of the Jedi* allowed Lucas to go back to—and improve upon—*Star Wars* while also completing his three-part story. Luke, Leia, Chewbacca, Lando, and the robots all return to the planet Tatooine, where *Star Wars* had started, to rescue the trapped Han Solo. Fans also got a chance to meet Jabba the Hut, the gangster who had been mentioned, but never seen, in *Star Wars*. And like the plot of *Star Wars*, the plot of *Jedi* is centered on stopping the construction of Darth Vader's powerful Death Star weapon,

*Lucas poses with the cast of* Return of the Jedi *and director Richard Marquand (far right).*

which would give the Empire total control of the galaxy. All of these elements resulted in a feeling of familiarity for the audience. They were seeing something new, and yet it felt familiar.

Lucas also used new advances in technology to thrill his audience. The speeder-bike scenes on Endor, the forest moon, stunned audiences with an almost theme-park-ride level of excitement. The special-effects people at ILM created this entire scene. The scenes were filmed with the redwoods in California as a backdrop, and the actors were added later in the studios. These scenes are a perfect example of Lucas's faith in technology. Although the technology had not existed when Lucas wrote the script, he was completely sure that the people at ILM could create it.

Again, Lucas did not want to direct the film. He brought in Richard Marquand, an English director. He also brought back Lawrence Kasdan to do the writing. Like the other *Star Wars* films, the actual creation of the movie was a collaborative process. Lucas, Kasdan, and Marquand spent long hours together discussing ideas that should be included and deciding how those ideas would be shown on the screen. Kasdan enjoyed the process with Lucas, "I liked George, and he was always under pressure—they were always starting movies before they had scripts." He was especially impressed with the way Lucas brought the story together. "George understood that you could integrate the effects into the story so that they formed part of the story in a way people had never really tried before."

By the time *Return of the Jedi* was released, there was little doubt of the film's success. After the first two films broke records at the box office,

*Lucas's characters gripped younger audiences.*

all of America was waiting to see how the story would end. Perhaps the most amazing part of *Return of the Jedi* is how true it is to Lucas's original story. Lucas never changed his vision for the films no matter how successful they became. He had an idea in 1975 that was not completed until 1983, but he stayed on track the entire time. The only question on most people's minds when they saw *Return of the Jedi* was, "When is he going to make more?" They would have to wait more than fifteen years for the answer.

# CHAPTER SIX

# THRILLING THE AUDIENCE

Lucas's fame was established with the *Star Wars* trilogy. But he has created other **icons** that have become a part of popular society besides Luke Skywalker and Darth Vader. Indiana Jones has become the model for young and old adventurers everywhere.

## A NONSTOP THRILL RIDE

Even while he was working on the exhausting task of writing the script for *Star Wars*, Lucas was thinking of other projects. He had always wanted to do an adventure movie like the cliffhanger serials he watched on television as a boy. He even had a character in mind—Indiana Smith (named after his dog, Indiana)—a college professor and archaeologist who battles Nazis while searching for lost treasures. (Lucas's interest in archaeology came from a course he took at Modesto Junior College.)

In 1975, he met with director Phil Kaufman and told him his idea. Kaufman suggested that they combine Lucas's idea with the legend of the Lost Ark of the Covenant. But Kaufman had to work on another project, and the idea for an adventure movie was put aside.

When *Star Wars* opened in 1977, Lucas went to Hawaii on vacation and invited his friend Steven Spielberg to join him. (They had first met at a student film festival where Lucas had won an award for *THX 1138:4EB*.) Lucas and Spielberg discussed Lucas's idea for an adventure film called *Raiders of the Lost Ark*. Lucas wanted to produce it, and he wanted Spielberg to direct it.

Lawrence Kasdan agreed to write the screenplay, and Michael Eisner, then president of Paramount, read over the script. With all its action and effects, Eisner was afraid the film would cost too much. It was planned to be shot in seven countries on three continents. But Lucas was frugal. His motto was: "We can do anything, and we can figure out how to do it for a price."

Spielberg wanted *Raiders* to be as nonstop and thrilling as a ride at an amusement park. Lucas wanted to be true to the style of 1930s serials. The two men have completely opposite approaches to making movies. Spielberg designs the shots and action as they happen, while Lucas creates his films in the editing room.

*To create* Raiders of the Lost Ark, *Lucas formed a creative partnership with Steven Spielberg.*

Spielberg suggested they change the name Indiana Smith to Indiana Jones, because he thought Smith sounded too common. Lucas imagined that Indiana Jones would be rebellious, but with some morals, a lot like Han Solo. "He has to be a person we can look up to," Lucas thought. "We're doing a role model for little kids, so we have to be careful. We need someone who's honest and true and trusting."

**"We're doing a role model for little kids, so we have to be careful. We need someone who's honest and true and trusting."**

At first, Spielberg envisioned Indiana as a little more sleazy, but they compromised on someone "like Harrison Ford" as Lucas described him. They wanted Ford's look, style, and manner. But when the time came for casting, Lucas was looking for an unknown. He had heard good things about Tom Selleck, then about to start work on the CBS television series, *Magnum P.I.* But when CBS learned that someone as great as Lucas was trying to get a hold of their actor, they held on tight, figuring that they had someone special.

Spielberg then suggested that they cast Harrison Ford himself. But Ford had appeared in five Lucasfilm productions, and Lucas wanted to try different actors. However, they finally decided that Ford was the best actor for the role.

*Although Lucas was originally interested in another actor, he agreed to cast Harrison Ford as Indiana Jones.*

Lucas had structured the story, created the characters, and set the tone for the movie. He described the plot as, "either he's chasing them, or they're chasing him." But once shooting began, Lucas's role was over for the time being. Spielberg was the director, and Lucas trusted his vision of the work. Lucas still supplied the brakes for some of Spielberg's grand ideas, however, just as he had for Coppola. At one point, Spielberg wanted to use two thousand Arab extras, and Lucas talked him down to six hundred.

The film was budgeted at $20 million and shot in only seventy-three days—two weeks under schedule. Once shooting was completed, Lucas still had a hand in *Raiders*. He had been given the right to the final cut of the film, so he and Marcia edited it. He used his skill to clean up the movie and make it tight, suspenseful, and humorous. His style clearly shows in *Star Wars* and *Raiders*. They seem like complex movies, but they can be easily understood by seven-year-olds.

*Raiders of the Lost Ark* became the largest-grossing film of 1981. It also led to the creation of a sequel, *Indiana Jones and the Temple of Doom* in 1984. Unlike *Raiders*, which took viewers to various spots all over the globe, *Doom* took place primarily in the Temple of Doom, a frightening place with fiery pits.

Lucas's writers from *American Graffiti*, Katz and Huyck, wrote the story. Huyck said that

"George wanted it to be really scary." It was thrilling, especially its ending sequences—the mining-car chase and the collapsing rope bridge.

But critics didn't love the second film as much as they loved the first. Some thought it had too

*In* Raiders of the Lost Ark, *Lucas created exciting, action-packed scenes. Here, Indiana Jones comes face to face with a deadly snake.*

many thrills, and gave no time to take a breath. But critics also noted Lucas's creativity. In a feature story, Richard Schickel wrote: "The whole Lucas emphasis is on special effects, on loading the film with optical tricks that can be created only in movies, [and this] . . . opens the audience's mind . . . to the connections between a seemingly simple tale and the richer realms of myth."

## AN INDUSTRY OF FRIENDS

Helping fellow workers in the industry has always been important to Lucas, and that can be seen in the movies he has created. He has said, "On the one hand I'm doing these huge productions and at the same time I'm helping on these little productions, for my friends. They're all interesting movies, movies that I cared about and wanted to see made one way or another. Some of them were small failures, some of them were huge failures, and some were extremely nice movies. But in most of the interviews with me, and even within the company, they're passed right over, as though they never existed. But those movies may be closer to what I am than *Star Wars*."

**"But those movies may be closer to what I am than *Star Wars*."**

With the success of his movies, Lucas was in a position to experiment with new techniques such as Lumage, a type of animation used in *Twice Upon a Time* in 1982. But most of his commitment was in helping young up-and-coming filmmakers, such as the Japanese filmmaker Akira Kurosawa with *Kagemusha* in 1980, or Larry Kasdan with his film *Body Heat* in 1981. In 1985, Lucas and Coppola joined forces as producers to help the young filmmaker Paul Schrader on *Mishima*. Lucas also was a part of Haskell Wexler's *Latino* in 1986.

Lucas greatly admired Jim Henson, the creator of the Muppets, and he was able to work with him on *Labyrinth* (1986). This film, the story of a girl who has to rescue her brother from a maze-like world, brought Lucasfilm and Henson Associates together as co-producers.

Lucas took his creativity in a new direction with *Captain EO* in 1986. It was created for the new three-dimensional Magic Eye Theater in Disneyland and the Epcot Center. Michael Jackson was the star, Lucas wrote the script, and Coppola directed. Its special effects were created at ILM.

One of Lucas's failures at the box office was *Howard the Duck* in 1986.

**"The Force was not with him."**

—Film critic

*Lucas worked with beloved muppet creator
Jim Henson to make the film* Labyrinth.

It was based on a comic book, and his writing team of Huyck and Katz were eager to write it. But the reviews were all terrible. One critic said that when Lucas made this film, "the Force was not with him."

*Willow*, in 1988, again gave Lucas a chance to show off his love of mythology. Set in the medieval past, the film was directed by Ron

Howard, who had been a cast member in *American Graffiti*.

Also in 1988, two other Lucas movies were released. He worked with Coppola on *Tucker: The Man and His Dream*. It told the story of Preston Tucker, a man who had tried to defy the major automobile manufacturers at the end of the World War II. He also joined forces with Spielberg again on *The Land Before Time*, an animated feature about a young dinosaur named Littlefoot.

Lucas's movie success enabled Lucasfilm to do some television production as well. The popularity of the *Star Wars* characters made big hits of *The Ewok Adventure: Caravan of Courage* and *Ewoks: The Battle for Endor*, both shown as "ABC Sunday Night Movies" in 1984 and 1985. Their success led to another spin-off—the animated-adventure series *Ewoks and Droids Adventure Hour*, which ran in the fall of 1985 and 1986.

## INDY RIDES AGAIN

In 1989, Lucas completed the Indiana Jones trilogy (though there are rumors that a fourth film is in the works) with *Indiana Jones and the Last Crusade*. Since some time had elapsed between *Doom* and *Last Crusade*, inflation and costs had shot up. While *Doom* had cost $30 million to create in 1984, *Crusade*'s budget was $44 million in 1989.

The story began as a Chinese legend about a Monkey King in Africa, but Lucas and Spielberg wanted something different. They decided to use the story of the quest for the Holy Grail. Like the other Indiana Jones movies, this one was filled with thrills.

The recognizability of Indiana Jones was so strong that Lucas developed him for the small screen as well. In 1992, the *Young Indiana Jones Chronicles* debuted on ABC. The series developed from Lucas's educational foundation, which is trying to develop interactive education and use television as a teaching device. In the *Young Indiana Jones Chronicles*, the hero enjoys both physical and intellectual adventures all over the world.

# CHAPTER SEVEN

# BACK TO THE WAR IN THE STARS

In 1997, the twentieth anniversary of *Star Wars'* first release, the true impact of *Star Wars* became obvious, even to those who had not realized it before. All three films were re-released in theaters as the *Star Wars Trilogy Special Edition—Star Wars* in January, *The Empire Strikes Back* in February, and *Return of the Jedi* in March. Not only were the films brought back for audiences to enjoy, but Lucas was given the chance to improve his original work.

Lucas had not been entirely happy with the films when they were first released. He now says that the original *Star Wars* "was about sixty percent of what I wanted it to be." He had ideas for creatures and special effects that could not be created in the 1970s and 1980s because he didn't have enough money or enough time, and because the technology wasn't advanced enough for the

*Twenty years after* Star Wars *was first released,
it was back in the movie theaters.*

effects to be believable. The re-release of the movies gave him the opportunity to add the finishing touches he had always hoped for.

## RESTORING A MASTERPIECE

The first step was to restore the original films. Although they had been stored in a safe place, the film had deteriorated, and the colors had faded. Each individual frame of the films was cleaned and brought back to perfect form. Lucas then added new effects. He included a new scene in *Star Wars* in which Han Solo meets Jabba the Hut. This sequence had to be cut out of the original film because Jabba could not be created to Lucas's satisfaction. With the new computer-imaging technology now available, Lucas was able to go back to the original footage and add in Jabba the Hut with computers. A scene that showed Harrison Ford talking to another actor now showed him arguing with the huge slug-like creature that previously appeared only in *Return of the Jedi*.

Lucas also added creatures to several scenes on Luke Skywalker's home planet of Tatooine and in the "monster" cantina. The space battles also became more spectacular, with computers allowing for more angles and more explosions. All three films underwent the same kinds of improvements. Lucas made no major changes in the movies, but he feels the new effects complete the picture of the world he was trying to create.

Along with the new special effects, Lucas also reworked the sound in the films. The *Special Edition* movies were not only better visually, but they offered an amazing sound experience. Lucas took a movie made in 1977 and brought it up to 1997 standards.

The ultimate test of the films came in the theaters. Lucas had spent $15 million to redo the movies. This was more money than it had cost to make *Star Wars* in 1977. Nobody could have predicted how successful the re-release of the movies would be. *Star Wars* was number one at the box office for four weeks and quickly passed the $100-million mark in earnings. *The Empire Strikes Back* and *Return of the Jedi* also premiered in the number-one spot and added millions in earnings. The public's anticipation of all three movies was unlike anything seen in years. Lucas was stunned by how much the reissue of the movie was like the first premiere of *Star Wars*. "It's like a revisiting of the entire event. I certainly didn't expect this to happen." Not only did the generation that had grown up with the films

**"It's like a revisiting of the entire event. I certainly didn't expect this to happen."**

*Lucas gathers with some familiar characters at the rerelease of* Star Wars *in 1997.*

return to enjoy them, but a whole new generation grew to love the movies as well. *Star Wars* merchandise filled the stores once again, including videocassettes of the movie that came out just in time for holiday sales. "It's nice to think of [the movies] as timeless," Lucas says.

## BACK TO THE BEGINNING

The summer of 1999 will see the return of Lucas's world to the big screen. *Star Wars: Episode 1* will be released, starting Lucas's return to the first three episodes in his nine-movie epic. These "prequels," or the movies that come before the three films that fans have already seen, will cover information fans have always wanted to know. How did Darth Vader become evil? Why did Obi-Wan Kenobi spend all those years hiding on Tatooine? What did Yoda do before he ended up on his swamp planet of Dagobah? What were the Clone Wars? Hopefully, Lucas will answer all of these questions along with many more in the next three films.

Lucas is taking a big step with the next trilogy. He is not only writing the new films, but he will also direct at least *Episode I*. This will be the first film Lucas has directed since the original *Star Wars*. We can be sure the films will also include an amazing array of new ships, characters, creatures, and effects. The additions to the *Star Wars Special Edition* were only a brief glimpse at how today's computer technology will change the look of *Star Wars*. We can be sure that Lucas will continue to push the edge of technology in filmmaking. We can also be certain that lines of moviegoers will wind around theaters just as they did back on that fateful day in May 1977.

# CHAPTER EIGHT

THE EMPIRE

Lucas has created three companies—LucasArts Entertainment Company, Lucas Digital Ltd., and Lucasfilm Ltd. Each company contributes to the entertainment industry in different ways.

## PLAYING GAMES WITH LUCASARTS

The LucasArts Entertainment Company is committed to teaching children. LucasArts Learning, established in 1978, provides schools and homes with computer programs for interactive teaching and learning. "If we can make these multimedia experiences interesting enough so that the child is the motivator, I think that's the most powerful way to learn," Lucas has said. LucasArts Games develops software for entertainment. Its most famous game was probably *Maniac Mansion* (which also became a television series in 1990).

Some of its most recent games include *Grim Fandango, X-wing vs. TIE Fighter, Star Wars Masters,* and *Herc's Adventures.*

## LUCAS DIGITAL SIGHTS AND SOUNDS

Lucas Digital Ltd. provides moviemakers with two of the most important elements in a movie—visual effects and sound design. It consists of two companies—Industrial Light and Magic (ILM) and Skywalker Sound.

ILM began when Lucas needed visual effects for *Star Wars.* Located in San Rafael, California, it is the best effects facility in the world today for the movie and television industries. ILM has won many Academy Awards for Best Visual Effects and Technical Achievement. Lucas once said, "In the first decade, the only time that ILM did not win an Academy Award for special effects was when it was matched against another ILM nominee that did win." Besides its famous work on the *Star Wars* movies, ILM has provided effects for many other films,

> **"The only time that ILM did not win an Academy Award for special effects was when it was matched against another ILM nominee that did win."**

*Lucas edits special effects.*

including, *Titanic, Men in Black, The Lost World, 101 Dalmatians, Mission Impossible*, and *Twister*.

Lucas works very closely with the designers at ILM, who not only create the sets, creatures, or ships for a special effect but also decide how the camera shots will look. Lucas believes strongly in the importance of preplanning, so designers plan every effect with storyboards. Artists sketch out the scenes of the entire movie and hang the sketches up on a wall. Then the papers can be rearranged, redesigned, or tossed out before millions of dollars are spent on a visual effect. ILM filled a five-hundred-page notebook with the storyboards for *The Empire Strikes Back* and a one-thousand-page notebook for *Return of the Jedi*.

Departments at ILM include:

- *Models:* After artists sketch ideas for models, model makers build small versions of a model for approval before a larger model is completed. For *Star Wars*, model makers built fewer than 50 models. For *The Empire Strikes Back,* they added slightly over 100. For *Return of the Jedi,* they built more than 160 new models.
- *Miniaturization:* Miniatures are used when there is an impossible situation to shoot (such as Indiana Jones riding in a mine car past molten lava in *Indiana Jones and the Temple of Doom*).
- *Creatures:* Creatures can be either human-size puppets, or stop-motion puppets that are filmed separately from the action.
- *Special Effects Animation:* Animators of special effects create certain parts of a film, such as Luke Skywalker's light saber.
- *Matte Painting:* If a location cannot be shot because it is too costly to travel there, or if

*Model builders of the original* Star Wars
*proudly display a number of their creations.*

it doesn't exist, a matte painting is used. A
matte painting is a large realistic painting
with an unpainted area. The filmed action
is later inserted. For example, the final
scene in *Raiders of the Lost Ark*, when a
man wheels a crate into a huge warehouse
filled with millions of other crates and

boxes, was a matte painting. The man and his crate are real, but the warehouse and the millions of boxes are a matte painting.

Skywalker Sound, which began as Sprocket Systems in 1980, is a postproduction company with three studios in California that provide movie-sound design. At Skywalker Sound, Lucas and his team designed new and better ways to make movie soundtracks. The postproduction at Skywalker Sound includes dialogue, sound effects, music, editing, and mixing. The films mixed by Skywalker Sound include all three *Star Wars* movies; all three *Indiana Jones* movies; *Terminator 2: Judgment Day; Jurassic Park; Forest Gump; Jumanji;* and *Mission Impossible.*

## THE AUDIENCE IS LISTENING

Lucas once said, "Sound is fifty percent of the motion picture experience." That thought led to the creation of the THX division of Lucasfilm Ltd. in 1983. Think about the last time you went to the movies. The movie is about to start, and a loud, rising, powerful noise fills the theater as the screen reads: "THX—The Audi-

**"Sound is fifty percent of the motion picture experience."**

ence is Listening." The THX Sound System is Lucas's invention, and it is installed in about one thousand theaters in the United States, and in another four hundred around the world.

In an interview with film critic Roger Ebert, Lucas said, "I've watched lots of movies under lots of different conditions, and how a film is presented has a great deal to do with your emotional response to that movie and how much you enjoy it, how much you get out of it. . . . We've discovered that twice as many people will go to a THX theater showing the same movie in the same city in the same-quality theater. . . . They want the best possible presentation."

Within the THX division, groups are designed to improve picture and sound in both the theater and the home. If a movie theater belongs to the THX Sound System Program, it must follow a rigorous set of rules in building a THX theater. The Home THX Program is developing technologies to reproduce the theater experience in the home.

# CHAPTER NINE

# THE MOVIEMAKING IDEAL

Lucas has always gone against the grain in Hollywood, and has proved that he can still be a success in the motion-picture industry. Film critic Leonard Maltin described Lucas's effect on movies when he said, "*Star Wars* may have started out as a mere movie . . . it changed the way movies were made." Part of this success can be attributed to how passionate Lucas is about moviemaking.

> **"*Star Wars* may have started out as a mere movie . . . it changed the way movies were made."**

"The focus of my life, the thing I care most about, was and is making movies: writing and shooting and editing films," Lucas has said.

## LUCAS'S THINK-RANCH

Making great movies has not been Lucas's only goal in life, however. He also believes that a creative work environment is important to filmmakers. So instead of just complaining about Hollywood, Lucas created a place called Skywalker Ranch. Spielberg describes Skywalker Ranch as "an extraordinary complex in Northern California, from where [Lucas] continues to stretch the limitations of education and entertainment."

Lucas says that the inspiration for Skywalker Ranch started in college. He saw USC as a model: "At that time the school was a tiny enclave of creative people working together and having everything we needed to make movies in a pleasant environment. It was quite a bit different from the way the studios were set up, like large factories."

The company that Lucas started with Coppola in 1969—American Zoetrope—was a step in this direction. When that experiment failed, Lucas filled notebooks with his ideas for another ideal moviemaking environment. In 1978, with money made from *American Graffiti* and *Star Wars*, Lucas bought property on Lucas Valley Road. It is just a coincidence that he and the road have the same name, but it may have been

*Lucas relaxes at Skywalker Ranch.*

fate that led him to the perfect place for Skywalker Ranch.

Construction began in 1980. While professional architects made the blueprints for Skywalker Ranch, Lucas designed the style,
placement, and details of the buildings. He wanted the buildings to feel as if they were a part of
the land—not intruding upon it. The buildings are
out of sight of each other, and cars are hidden

away in underground garages. "What I wanted to build," he says, "was a work environment that is a model of the way I think creative people should be allowed to work."

Since Lucas believes "writers need the support of a large research library," Skywalker Ranch is complete with a large library—including books about Egypt, India, and the Crusades used for the *Indiana Jones* films. It is also home to some of Lucas's companies, where a lot of postproduction work is done—not only on Lucas's movies, but on the movies of other filmmakers.

**"What I wanted to build was a work environment that is a model of the way I think creative people should be allowed to work."**

## HAVING THE FORCE

In an October 1997 issue of *Entertainment Weekly*, Lucas was named the sixth most powerful person in Hollywood. But even though he is a multimillionaire and creative genius, Lucas is still a very normal person who usually dresses in jeans and sneakers. "I'm so ordinary," he says about himself, "that a lot of people can relate to me, because it's the same kind of ordinary that they are. I think it gives me an insight into the mass audience. I know what I liked as a kid, and I still like it."

**"I'm so ordinary that a lot of people can relate to me, because it's the same kind of ordinary that they are."**

The *Star Wars* trilogy has become a part of modern culture. And the number of fans keeps growing. Anxious for the release of *The Empire Strikes Back,* 130,000 people called a toll-free number—in one day—to find out more about it. (It was enough to short-circuit the switchboard!) More recently, fans have visited a ride at Disney's MGM Studios called Star Tours, where a robot takes the audience on a galactic *Star Wars* adventure. At the National Air and Space Museum in Washington, D.C., a special exhibit displayed more than two hundred *Star Wars* items from the Lucasfilm Archives.

Lucas does not take the power he has over his audiences lightly. Children are often his main audience, and now as a divorced father of three children (two through adoption), Lucas can watch his movies through their eyes. Lucas tries to create an ideal world where good always wins over evil. We even find that Darth Vader, one of the most dreaded villains in history, is actually a "good guy" in the end. During his acceptance speech of the Irving G. Thalberg Award from the

*Lucas's ranch in Nicasto, California*

Academy of Motion Picture Arts and Sciences in 1992, Lucas said, "I've always tried to be aware of what I say in my films because all of us who make motion pictures are teachers; teachers with very loud voices."

From the time he was a child reading adventure comic books to his present-day fame and fortune, it cannot be disputed that the Force has always been with George Lucas.

*Lucas takes his power over popular culture and young people very seriously. Here, he attends a movie premiere with his daughter Amanda.*

# CHRONOLOGY

| | |
|---|---|
| 1944 | George Walton Lucas, Jr., is born on May 14. |
| 1962 | Lucas is injured in a severe car accident on June 12; graduates from Thomas Downey High School. |
| 1964 | Lucas graduates from Modesto Junior College. |
| 1966 | Lucas graduates from the University of Southern California (USC) film school. |
| 1967 | Lucas meets Steven Spielberg at a student film festival. |
| 1968 | Lucas goes back to USC for one semester as a graduate student; wins a scholarship to observe the making of *Finian's Rainbow* at Warner Brothers studio and meets Francis Ford Coppola; makes *Filmmaker* (writer, director, photographer, editor). |
| 1969 | Lucas marries Marcia Griffin on February 22; American Zoetrope founded. |
| 1971 | Lucas's first feature film, *THX 1138*, released (Lucas as co-writer, director, and editor). |

| 1972 | Lucasfilm Ltd. created. |
|------|------------------------|
| 1973 | *American Graffiti* released (Lucas as co-writer and director). |
| 1975 | Industrial Light and Magic founded. |
| 1977 | *Star Wars* released (Lucas as writer and director). Wins Academy Awards for best original score, best film editing, best art and set decoration, best costume design, and best visual effects. |
| 1979 | *More American Graffiti* released (Lucas as executive producer). |
| 1980 | Skywalker Sound created (began as Sprocket Systems); *The Empire Strikes Back* released (Lucas as executive producer) and wins Academy Award for best sound. |
| 1981 | *Raiders of the Lost Ark* released (Lucas as co-executive producer) and wins Academy Awards for best art direction, best sound, best film editing, and best visual effects. |
| 1982 | *Twice Upon a Time* released (Lucas as executive producer). |
| 1983 | THX division of Lucasfilm Ltd. created; *Return of the Jedi* released (Lucas as executive producer and co-writer). |
| 1984 | *Indiana Jones and the Temple of Doom* released (Lucas as co-executive producer) and wins Academy Award for best visual effects; *The Ewok Adventure: Caravan of Courage* airs on television (Lucas as executive producer) and wins an Emmy for outstanding special effects. |
| 1985 | *Ewoks: The Battle for Endor* airs on television (Lucas as executive producer) and wins an Emmy for outstanding special effects. |

| 1985 | *Mishima* released (Lucas as co-executive producer). |
|------|-------|
| 1986 | *Labyrinth* released (Lucas as executive producer); *Howard the Duck* released (Lucas as executive producer); *Captain EO* first shown in Disneyland and Epcot Center (Lucas as executive producer and writer). |
| 1987 | LucasArts Learning established. |
| 1988 | *Willow* released (Lucas as executive producer); *Tucker: The Man and His Dream* released (Lucas as executive producer). |
| 1989 | *Indiana Jones and the Last Crusade* released (Lucas as co-executive producer) and wins Academy Award for best sound-effects editing. |
| 1990 | Home THX program introduced. |
| 1992 | *The Young Indiana Jones Chronicles* debuts on television (Lucas as executive producer); Lucas receives the Irving G. Thalberg Award from the Academy of Motion Picture Arts and Sciences. |
| 1993 | THX Digital Mastering Program introduced, dealing with video, laser discs, and DVD discs; *Jurassic Park* released (Lucas as editor). |
| 1994 | *Radioland Murders* released (Lucas as executive producer and writer). |
| 1997 | *Star Wars, The Empire Strikes Back*, and *Return of the Jedi Special Editions* are released to commemorate the twentieth anniversary of *Star Wars*. |
| 1999 | *Star Wars: Episode I* released (Lucas as director, executive producer, and writer). |

# GLOSSARY

**cinematographer**  the person in charge of running the camera and filming the movie

**crew**  all of the people involved in the making of a movie

**diabetes**  a disorder in which the body cannot use sugar properly

**director**  the person in charge of every aspect of a film

**documentary**  a nonfiction film meant to be educational

**editor**  a person who cuts and rearranges film or text into its final form

**grip**  the person in charge of props and carrying film equipment

**icon**  a character that people admire

**postproduction**  the addition of sound, music, and special effects after a movie has been filmed

**science fiction**  a story involving setting, characters, or technology that does not exist

**score**  the music created for a movie

**serial**   a story divided into several parts and told over a period of time

**special effects**   ways of making unreal or impossible situations believable

**trilogy**   a series of three films or three books

# A NOTE ON SOURCES

While researching information for this book, Chris and Dana Rau found it was the perfect time to be doing a biography on George Lucas. With the release of the *Star Wars* Special Editions both in theaters and video cassette in 1997, and the all-new *Star Wars* movie in 1999, Lucas was often in the news. The authors used news articles, such as those found in *Time, Newsweek,* and *Entertainment Weekly*, movie reviews, and even an interview on *Oprah Winfrey* as current sources.

To find out about Lucas's life as a youth, student, and filmmaker, the authors found *Skywalking: The Life and Films of George Lucas* to be invaluable. Another source that provided a wealth of information was *George Lucas—The Creative Impulse: Lucasfilm's First Twenty Years,* which discussed the structure of his company, Lucasfilm Ltd., as well as each of Lucas's movies.

After wading through piles of books, they found that in order to get the most up-to-date information, websites were the best place to visit. Here, they found articles by Lucas himself about his past works and future projects. While this fast-paced technology proved helpful, the authors found it fun to find some old sources, too, such as the old, beat-up *Star Wars* book buried deep in Chris's closet that he bought back in 1977 when he was only six years old.

# FOR MORE INFORMATION

## BOOKS

Carrau, Bob. *Monsters and Aliens from George Lucas.* New York: Harry N. Abrams, Inc., 1993.

Champlin, Charles. *George Lucas: The Creative Impulse—Lucasfilm's First Twenty Years.* New York: Harry N. Abrams, Inc., 1992.

Pollock, Dale. *Skywalking: The Life and Films of George Lucas.* New York: Harmony Books, 1983.

Pye, Michael, and Linda Myles. *The Movie Brats: How a Film Generation Took over Hollywood.* Texas: Holt, Rinehart, and Winston, 1984.

Smith, Thomas G. *Industrial Light and Magic: The Art of Special Effects.* New York: Ballantine Books, 1986.

## INTERNET RESOURCES

The George Lucas Educational Foundation
**http://glef.org**
Created as a result of Lucas's belief in education's vital

importance to society, the George Lucas Educational Foundation offers students, teachers, and communities information about ways to use interactive multimedia technologies to transform teaching and learning.

LucasArts Entertainment Company
**http://www.lucasarts.com**
Find out about the latest CD-ROM games and software coming from LucasArts, and read their newsletter, *The Adventurer*.

The Official *Star Wars* Web Site
**http://www.starwars.com/**
This site changes on a regular basis, bringing visitors the most up-to-date information on the latest *Star Wars* news.

The THX Home Page
**http://www.thx.com**
This website describes what the THX division of Lucasfilm Ltd. is doing in sound innovations for theaters and the home.

# INDEX

Page numbers in *italics* indicate illustrations.

▲ 110 ▲

# ABOUT THE AUTHORS

Even when they were kids, Chris and Dana Rau loved the movies. They loved the feel of movie-theater seats and the smell of butter-soaked popcorn. Among Chris's favorite movies of all time were all three *Star Wars* films, and among Dana's were all three *Indiana Jones* films. So when Chris and Dana met in college, they discovered that they were the perfect match. Not only did they sometimes see up to five movies in a weekend, like Lucas himself, but they also joined forces to write the weekly movie review in the college's newspaper. This was the best movie deal they will ever have—someone paid them to see a movie a week!

Today, Chris is an eighth-grade social studies teacher, and Dana is a children's book writer and editor. They live in Farmington, Connecticut. Someday, when they have lots and lots of money, they plan to build a THX theater in their home and decorate the walls with their movie posters and all of the ticket stubs Dana has saved over the years.